靜思精舍惜物造福的智慧故事❶

感恩
穀粉的故事

總策劃 / 靜思書軒

**The Wisdom of Cherishing and Sowing Blessings
at the Jing Si Abode (I)
Gratitude: The Story of Jing Si Multi-Grain Instant Mix**

五穀
粉

「媽，我下課了！」

「小恩回來啦！會餓嗎？你要不要試試看我新買的穀粉。」媽媽說：「是用天然的豆穀做成，營養很豐富喔。」

媽媽沖泡的穀粉聞起來有股淡雅的香氣，小恩喝完覺得很飽足，梳洗完畢，就進房間寫功課。

"Mom, I'm home from school!"

"Oh, Xiao-En, you're home! Are you hungry? Do you want to try this Multi-Grain Instant Mix I bought?" Xiao-En's mother said, "It's made from natural soybean and grains, and it's very nutritious!"

Xiao-En's mother mixed the Multi-Grain Instant Mix with hot water, creating a mixture that smelled light and heavenly. Xiao-En felt very full after drinking it. He then washed up and went into his room to do his homework.

　　小恩寫完功課，睡覺之前問媽媽：「今天喝的穀粉好好喝喔！是在哪裏買的呢？」

　　媽媽回答：「你今天喝的穀粉是靜思精舍最早和大家分享的結緣物，早期叫做豆元粉（薏豆粉）。」

　　「媽媽，靜思精舍的師父們為什麼想做穀粉和大家結緣呢?」

Xiao-En later finished his homework, but before he went to sleep, he asked his mother, "That Multi-Grain Instant Mix I had today was delicious! Where did you buy it?"

Xiao-En's mother replied, "That Multi-Grain Instant Mix was one of the earliest gifts that the Dharma Masters at the Jing Si Abode would give to visitors. It used to be called 'dou yuan powder.'"

"But mom, why did the Dharma Masters at the Jing Si Abode want to make Multi-Grain Instant Mix as gifts?"

「有一位營養學家建議精舍師父把多種豆類爆開，磨成粉沖泡，讓證嚴上人補充營養。上人飲用後覺得精神和身體都得到能量，問可否大量生產做成產品，不但可以和大家分享，靜思精舍也能藉此自力更生。明白上人的心願後，師父們開始試做和大量生產的計畫。」媽媽說。

Xiao-En's mother explained, "A nutritionist suggested that the resident masters could roast the soybean and grains, grind it into powder, and serve it in hot water. This would benefit Dharma Master Cheng Yen's health and nutrition. After the Dharma Master tried it, she felt that her spirit and body were both refreshed. She asked if more of the powder could be made, so that it could be shared with more people, and might even be used to help support the Jing Si Abode. The Dharma Masters at the Abode understood what Dharma Master Cheng Yen was hoping for, and they started planning to make lots of powder."

為了滿足小恩對穀粉製作的好奇心，於是媽媽帶著小恩前往花蓮靜思精舍參觀。

　　「哇！這是哪裡？」小恩說。

　　「這裡是靜思精舍。」媽媽很興奮的說：「小恩你看，師父們坐在那裡做什麼？」

　　「哇！他們在選豆子嗎？」小恩說。

　　「師父們正在細心挑選豆子，這是製作穀粉的第一步。」媽媽說。

Because Xiao-En was so curious about how the Multi-Grain Instant Mix is made, Xiao-En's mother brought him to the Jing Si Abode in Hualien to see for himself.

"Wow! What's this place?" Xiao-En asked.

"This is the Jing Si Abode," Xiao-En's mother replied excitedly. "Look, do you see what the Dharma Masters sitting there are doing?"

"Are they sorting the beans?" Xiao-En replied.

"Yes, the Dharma Masters are carefully sorting the beans. This is the first step for making the Multi-Grain Instant Mix." said Xiao-En's mother.

穀粉是從豆穀的挑揀、清洗、瀝乾，充分晾曬後，再倒入鍋爐翻炒、乾爆，膨發成熟料。再經過磨粉、裝袋、運銷，就成為補充體力的營養品。每個環節都充滿師父和志工們的細心照料。

To make the Multi-Grain Instant Mix, the beans are first sorted, cleaned, drained, and sun-dried. Then they are fried and roasted in a cooker until they expand and are cooked through. Finally, they are ground into powder, packaged and transported. The nutritious and energetic treat is made by Dharma Masters and volunteers, who are always very careful every step of the way.

師父們在清洗烤盤和烤架。

媽媽指著靜思精舍前庭說：「以前晴天的時候，豆穀會放在這從早曬到晚；快下雨時，師父們會很快的把豆穀搬進來，不讓豆穀受到雨淋。」

小恩說：「師父們把豆穀照顧得好好哦！」

Xiao-En's mother pointed at the courtyard in front of the Abode and said, "In the past, on sunny days, the beans would be sun-dried from morning to night.
But when it's about to rain,
Dharma Masters would quickly move the
beans indoors so that they would
not get wet."

Xiao-En said, "The Dharma
Masters take such
good care of the beans!"

13

曬豆之後要炒豆，「什麼時候加柴火」是豆穀香甜的秘訣。主掌的師父要用心聽出爐中聲音的變化，再決定什麼時候加粗的柴火，還是細的柴火。

　　小恩說：「這個『聽出來』的工夫很厲害啊！」

Adding firewood to the cooker at the right time was the key to making the best roasted beans. The Dharma Master in charge would listen closely to the sound of the beans in the cooker to decide when to add large pieces of wood, and when to add small ones.

Xiao-En said, "It's incredible she used her hearing to help her roast the beans !"

15

16

「您們好，歡迎回家。這是第一代爆粉的機器，是跟停業的爆米花攤販買的，機器老舊，高溫運轉時容易產生氣爆，噴在皮膚上又燙又痛，傷口結痂後還會留疤。」德安師父說。

媽媽心疼的說：「爆粉要很小心啊！」

"Hello! Welcome! This is the first type of cooker we used in the Abode. We bought it from a popcorn seller. It was quite old, which meant it might explode when we used it. It would burn our skin painfully when it exploded, leaving wounds and scars." Dharma Master De An said.

Xiao-En's mother said with concern, "You must be careful when roasting the beans!"

18

德安師父說起印象特別深刻的爆粉往事：「有一次，機器上的橡皮壞了，我在忙所以不知道，但離爆粉間50公尺外的上人，已經聞到和平常不一樣的味道。上人要德恩師父過來關心，我才說沒事，一轉身，火已經冒了兩尺高！」

Dharma Master De An recalled a particularly memorable explosion, "Once, the rubber on the machine was worn, but I was too busy to notice. But Dharma Master Cheng Yen, who was 50 meters away from the workshop, could smell something unusual. She sent Dharma Master De En over to check on it. I looked, and then said it was fine, but as soon as I turned around, flames two feet high started shooting out of the cooker!"

「我是用布袋沾水滅火。因為忙著滅火，機器上設定膨爆的時間已經超過了，溫度持續升高。突然『碰！』一聲，屋頂燒成焦黑，為了保護其他人，我用身體阻擋機器爆衝造成的強大撞擊，手腳腫脹瘀青，胸口也因為撞擊，連說話、呼吸都會痛。」

"I tried putting out the fire with a wet cloth sack, but because I was so busy with the fire, I didn't notice that it was past the cooker's pre-set cooking time. Since we hadn't stopped the cooker, the temperature continued rising until... boom! Even the ceiling was burned black! I tried to protect the others by blocking the exploding cooker with my body. It caused bruises and swelling on my arms and legs, and my chest was injured so badly it hurt to even talk or breathe."

德安師父說：「很感恩會眾與訪客的護持，我們每天趕工，把工廠當道場。上人說：『唸經千遍，不如做一遍。』不工作的人就是『四等公民』—— 等吃、等睡、等玩、等死。不做『四等公民』是我們的工作哲學。」

Dharma Master De An said, "We're thankful to the visitors for their support. Because we're working so hard every day, the workshop has become our place of cultivation. As Dharma Master Cheng Yen said, 'Taking action is better than reading sutras a thousand times.' Those who do not work are not using their time meaningfully; they eat, they sleep, they play, and finally they die. We are determined to use our time meaningfully; this is what drives us to work."

「您們好，歡迎回家！」

「請問爆粉間是師父管理的嗎？」小恩問。

「是啊，我每天早上六點半，就來到爆粉間開機、工作。上人期許我要照顧好同仁們的安全，同時，不要讓大家在體力上太勞累。」德偌師父說。

"Hello! Welcome!"

"Dharma Master, are you in charge of the workshop?" Xiao-En asked.

"Indeed! At 6:30 every morning, I come to the workshop to turn on the cooker and start the work. When we started working at this new workshop, Dharma Master Cheng Yen specifically asked us to take care of the safety of all the workers, and to make sure no one gets too tired," Dharma Master De Ruo replied.

「這裡有好大的機器喔！」小恩說。

「為了讓穀粉和更多人分享，我們決定增加產量，在2014年搬到靜思精舍旁邊的協力工廠。」

媽媽說：「這是機械化的好處，可以大量生產。」

"There's a big machine here!" Xiao-En exclaimed.

"We wanted to make more Multi-Grain Instant Mix and share it with more people, so in 2014 we moved to a new workshop across from the Abode."

Xiao-En's mother said, "That's the great thing about using machines. You can make lots of the product."

小恩問：「請問師父，您是機器專家嗎？」

德偌師父說：「我不是專家，因為小時候家裡很窮，小學畢業後就去織布廠工作。如果織布機故障，自己想辦法找出原因，解決問題，日子久了，對機器愈來愈熟悉。」

小恩說：「好厲害，無師自通。」

Xiao-En asked, "Dharma Master, are you an expert in the machines?"

Dharma Master De Ruo replied, "No, I'm not an expert. I grew up poor, so after I graduated from elementary school, I started working at a textile factory. When the machines that weaved textiles broke down, I would do my best to find the problem and fix it. After a while, I became familiar with the machines."

Xiao-En said in admiration, "That's amazing. You taught yourself!"

「來，休息一下，請你們喝杯穀粉。對機器來講，聽聲音是很重要的。上人有一句話是『用寧靜的心，觀看眾生相』，我是用很寧靜的心去聽，哪裡聲音不對勁，從中判斷問題，進行維修。」

媽媽說：「師父把機器當作菩薩，用修行的心修理機器啊！」

"Come, take a break and enjoy a cup of Multi-Grain Instant Mix. It's important for us to listen to the sounds of the machines. Dharma Master Cheng Yen once said, 'With a tranquil mindset, observe the appearances of all sentient beings.' I listen closely with this tranquil mindset. When I hear something unusual, I can diagnose the problem and fix it."

Xiao-En's mother said, "Dharma Master treats the machine like a Bodhisattva and treats fixing machines as spiritual practice."

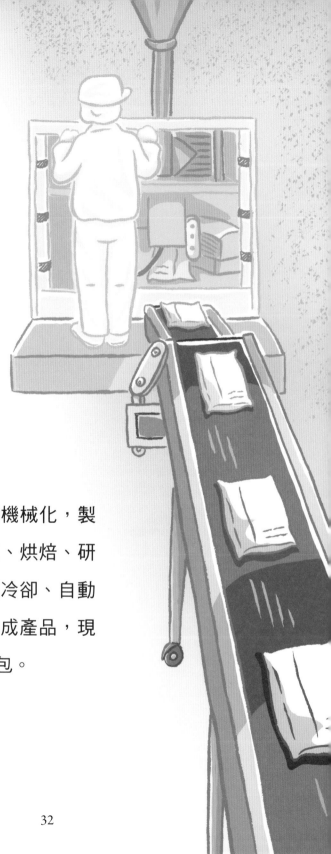

　　設備目前都已經機械化，製作過程從膨發、炒豆、烘焙、研磨，變成粉後再經過冷卻、自動翻轉、攪拌，再包裝成產品，現在30分鐘就能產出一包。

The ingredients for the Multi-Grain Instant Mix are grown locally on small farms in Hualien, run by indigenous farmers. The workshop now uses machines fully through the entire process, from expanding (rehydrate), cooking, roasting, and grinding the beans to automatic cooling, turning, mixing, and packaging. One bag of Multi-Grain Instant Mix can be made in just 30 minutes.

德倻師父說：「我一直在思考，做生產穀粉這件事，這樣算是修行嗎？但是被各種事物考驗時，才深深體會到上人說的『藉事練心，藉境修行』，以感恩的心來看待這件事，才能面對考驗，解決問題，這也是一種修行，上人的話真有遠見！」

Dharma Master De Ruo said, "I often wonder if making Multi-Grain Instant Mix can be considered a type of cultivation. But after handling so many challenges, I finally understood what Dharma Master Cheng Yen meant when she said, 'Train your mind with work, and cultivate with your environment.' I choose to look at my work with gratitude, as it helps me tackle challenges and solve problems. This is also a type of cultivation. Dharma Master Cheng Yen's words are very wise!"

　　穀粉從手工製作到機器生產，在德慈、德安、德
佑三位師父不怕苦、不怕難、不做「四等公民」的堅持
下，勇於承擔、接受考驗，還保有一顆感恩的心，十分
可貴啊！」

　　「媽媽，我的名字有個『恩』字，我會好好珍惜和
感恩，向師父們看
齊！」小恩說。

"The Multi-Grain Instant Mix started out hand-made, and eventually was produced by machines. Dharma Masters De Ci, De An, and De Ruo were not discouraged by the hard work and difficulties, and were determined to use their time meaningfully. They shouldered the responsibility and handled the challenges, and kept a grateful heart. This is very rare and precious!"

"Mom, my name also has the character 'En'," which means gratitude! I will do my best to be like the Dharma Masters who make the Multi-Grain Instant Mix!" Xiao-En said.

一起動手做做看
Let's try making it!

看完精采的穀粉故事，一起動手來做五穀粉小餅乾和可可小餅乾，好看、好玩又好吃。

Now that we've learned about the Multi-Grain Instant Mix, let's try making cereal cookies and cocoa cookies. They're fun to make and yummy to eat!

五穀粉小餅乾（**12 個**）
Cereal Cookies（makes 12）

材料 Ingredients

五穀粉	30 克	30g of Multi-grain Instant Mix
燕麥薏仁風味粉	15 克	15g of Oats and Job's Tears Instant Mix
食用油	7 克	7g of cooking oil
熱水	12 克	12g of hot water

① 取一適當的容器，加入
粉料，放入油、水攪拌
均勻，再用手搓成團。

Add the instant mix powders, oil, and water to a suitable
container and mix thoroughly.Then knead the mixture
into a dough.

② 粉團以掌心壓平，再用桿麵棍桿平。

Press the dough flat with
your palms, and flatten it
with a roller.

③ 取出模具，壓出形狀備用。

Cut the dough into cookie
shapes with cookie cutters.

④ 將成型的餅乾放在烤盤上，以 150℃、
正反面各烘烤 5 分鐘（總共 10 分鐘）
即成。

Place the cookies on a baking tray, then
bake in a 150°C oven for 5 minutes on each
side, 10 minutes total.

可可小餅乾（**12 個**）

Cocoa Cookies（makes 12）

材料 Ingredients

五穀粉	20 克	20g of Multi-grain Instant Mix
燕麥薏仁風味粉	15 克	15g of Oats and Job's Tears Instant Mix
可可風味粉	10 克	10g of Cocoa Flavored Instant Mix
食用油	6 克	6g of cooking oil
熱水	12 克	12g of hot water

作法 Instructions

❶ 取一適當的容器，加入各式粉料，放入油、水攪拌均勻，再用手搓成團。

Add the instant mix powders, oil, and water to a suitable container and mix thoroughly, and knead the mixture into a dough.

❷ 粉團以掌心壓平，再用桿麵棍桿平。

Press the dough flat with your palms, and then flatten it with a roller.

壓

桿平

壓

❸ 取出模具，壓出形狀備用。

Cut the dough into cookie shapes with cookie cutters.

❹ 將成型的餅乾放在烤盤上，以 150℃、正反面各烘烤 5 分鐘（總共 10 分鐘）即成。

150℃ 烤

正面5分鐘/反面5分鐘

Place the cookies on a baking tray, and then bake in a 150°C oven for 5 minutes on each side, 10 minutes total.

注意事項 Important Note

壓模時，可選用較小的模具，搭配五穀小餅乾的粉團，把餅乾中間的部分交換，做一點變化，造型更多元。

When cutting the dough, you can use smaller cookie cutters to make smaller cookies that can be combined with the dough from the cereal cookies, making cookies with combined flavors.

靜思語：感恩

感恩他人就是美化自己。

In showing gratitude, we become a more beautiful person.

《中英對照靜思小語 4》 | 《小學生 365 靜思語》

用感恩的心送走過去，用虔誠的心迎接未來。

Let us see the past off with gratitude and
welcome the future with a sincere heart.

《中英對照靜思小語 4》 | 《小學生 365 靜思語》

付出，才能有愛與感恩的互動。

It is through giving that people can
interact with one another with love
and gratitude.

《中英對照靜思小語 4》 | 《小學生 365 靜思語》

感恩可以打開我們的心結，並且啟發我們的悲心。

Having gratitude can help us dissolve our inner afflictions and inspire our compassion.

《中英對照靜思小語 4》｜《小學生 365 靜思語》

受人批評，應感恩對方。

When we are criticized by someone,
we should actually be grateful to that person.

《中英對照靜思小語 4》｜《小學生 365 靜思語》

關於穀粉

給老師和家長們更多關於淨皂的資訊。

 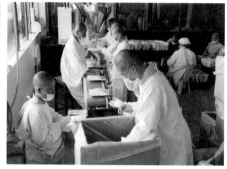

圖為師父正在調整機械化的穀粉設備。　圖為師父正在進行穀粉包裝的工作。
（攝影者：黃筱哲）

　　穀粉製作的因緣，源自高雄有位研究營養學的專家，感於證嚴上人為佛教、為眾生而日日忙碌，為強健上人體魄、補足營養，因此教導常住眾將多種穀類膨發、磨粉及混合後，沖泡成美味又營養的飲品予上人食用。鑑及此款飲品營養甚豐，不僅能增強抵抗力，也能增益腸胃功能，遂萌念能與大眾分享。穀粉自 1984 年試做，經謹慎研發、不斷改善，於一年後開始流通，是為靜思精舍深富歷史傳統與意義的自製食品；以其風味香醇、衛生營養，故甫推出即深受好評、口碑卓著，至今依然廣得社會大眾喜愛與歡迎。

　　找時間走訪一趟「靜思書軒」門市就可以找到穀粉，吃出健康和營養！

靜思人文
JING SI CULTURE

靜思精舍惜物造福的智慧故事 1

感恩：穀粉的故事

總 策 劃 / 靜思書軒
編　　審 / 釋德倍
照片提供 / 慈濟基金會文史處
故　　事 / 羅文翠
插　　圖 / 王佩娟
美術設計 / 羅吟軒
英　　譯 / Linguitronics Co., Ltd. 萬象翻譯（股）公司（故事及主題延伸）

總 編 輯 / 李復民
副總編輯 / 鄧懿貞
特約主編 / 陳佳聖
封面設計 / Javick 工作室
專案企劃 / 蔡孟庭、盤惟心

讀書共和國出版集團 業務平台
總經理 / 李雪麗　　　　　　副總經理 / 李復民
海外業務總監 / 張鑫峰　　　特販業務總監 / 陳綺瑩
零售資深經理 / 郭文弘　　　專案企劃總監 / 蔡孟庭
印務協理 / 江域平　　　　　印務主任 / 李孟儒

出　　版 / 發光體文化 / 遠足文化事業股份有限公司
發　　行 / 遠足文化事業股份有限公司（讀書共和國出版集團）
地　　址 / 231 新北市新店區民權路 108 之 2 號 9 樓
電　　話 / (02) 2218-1417　傳眞 / (02) 8667-1065
電子信箱 / service@bookrep.com.tw
網　　址 / www.bookrep.com.tw
郵撥帳號 / 19504465 遠足文化事業股份有限公司

法律顧問 / 華洋法律事務所 蘇文生律師
印　　製 / 凱林彩印股份有限公司

慈濟人文出版社
地　　址 / 臺北市忠孝東路三段二一七巷七弄十九號一樓
電　　話 / (02) 2898-9888
傳　　眞 / (02) 2898-9889
網　　址 / www.jingsi.org

2024 年 5 月 2 日初版一刷　　　定價 / 320 元
ISBN / 978-626-98109-4-9（精裝）　書號 / 2IGN1005

國家圖書館出版品預行編目 (CIP) 資料

靜思精舍惜物造福的智慧故事 . 1, 感恩 : 穀粉的故事 =
The wisdom of cherishing and sowing blessings at the
Jing Si Abode. 1, gratitude : the story of cereal powder
/ 羅文翠故事 . -- 初版 . -- 新北市 : 遠足文化事業股份有限
公司發光體文化 , 遠足文化事業股份有限公司 , 2024.04
　　面 ;　公分
中英對照
ISBN 978-626-98109-4-9(精裝)

224.515　　　　　　　　　　113003668